Speaking Our Language

Story by Jared Thomas
Illustrations by Alisha Monnin

Speaking Our Language

Text: Jared Thomas
Publishers: Tania Mazzeo and Eliza Webb
Series consultant: Amanda Sutera
  Hands on Heads Consulting
Editor: Kirsty Hine
Project editor: Annabel Smith
Project designer: Danielle Maccarone
Designer: Jess Kelly
Illustrations: Alisha Monnin
Production controller: Renee Tome

NovaStar

Text © 2024 Cengage Learning Australia Pty Limited
Illustrations © 2024 Cengage Learning Australia Pty Limited

ISBN 978 0 17 033435 8

Cengage Learning Australia
Level 5, 80 Dorcas Street
Southbank VIC 3006 Australia
Phone: 1300 790 853
Email: aust.nelsonprimary@cengage.com

For learning solutions, visit **cengage.com.au**

Printed in China by 1010 Printing International Ltd
1 2 3 4 5 6 7 28 27 26 25 24

*Nelson acknowledges the Traditional Owners and Custodians
of the lands of all First Nations Peoples. We pay respect
to Elders past and present, and extend that respect to
all First Nations Peoples today.*

Contents

Author's Note

I wrote this story because learning and speaking Nukunu (say: nook-oo-noo) language is important to my Nukunu family members, including my three daughters. We know that language helps us as Nukunu people to remember our culture and important things about the land. Nukunu names tell us about the types of plants and animals that belong in certain places on Country.

Nukunu Words

Here is a list of some of the Nukunu words that appear in this book and what they mean.

kartla (*gud-la*) – fire

Maama (*mar-ma*) – Dad

manarta (*mun-ar-da*) – big

Ngami (*nyum-me*) – Mum

nhakutya (*nar-car-jar*) – to see

nhiina (*nee-in-a*) – you

nyuntyi (*nyoon-tji*) – liar

purtlis (*pur-lees*) – stars

tyukarti (*tjook-ar-di*) – yes

wapma (*wob-ma*) – snake

warrarla (*warrar-la*) – language

yirityi (*yirit-gee*) – blue swimmer crabs

yirtas (*yid-ahs*) – birds

Nukunu Country Map

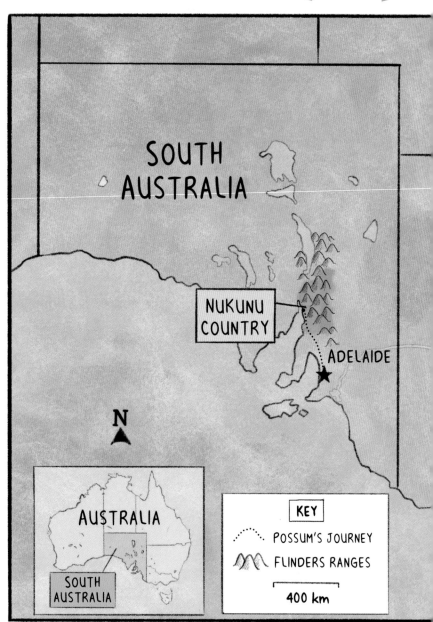

SOUTH
AUSTRALIA

NUKUNU
COUNTRY

ADELAIDE

N

AUSTRALIA

SOUTH
AUSTRALIA

KEY

········ POSSUM'S JOURNEY

FLINDERS RANGES

400 km

Chapter 1

Home to Country

I was so excited to
travel home to the
Flinders Ranges with
Ngami and Maama
(Mum and Dad) to
go camping. My
uncles and aunties,
cousins, and even
great-uncles and great-aunties were going
to camp with us too. It was going to be
so much fun.

When we arrived at the campground
near the coast, but also not far from the
ranges, everyone was gathered around
the kartla (fire), with swags and tents and
things laid out across our camp.

We jumped out of our car, and everyone came over to hug and greet us.

"Nhiina wanypatha?" asked Uncle Jack, and Maama replied, "Tyukarti, ngayi wanypatha."

It made me realise that I had to search my memory bank to remember all the Nukunu words that I used, because sometimes I get lazy and don't speak my language much when I'm in the city, where I live. *What did Maama and Uncle Jack just say?* I asked myself, and then I remembered that Uncle Jack had asked, "Are you well?" and Maama replied, "Yes, I'm good."

My Aunty Janey gave me the biggest hug, and I felt so happy wrapped up in her big soft warmth and she wouldn't stop kissing me on the cheeks and saying, "You've got so manarta, Pirlta, my little Possum." I liked it when my family called me by my Nukunu name, Pirlta, meaning possum, rather than just calling me Possum like the city folk do, because they find Pirlta too hard to say. "Pill-da," I explain to them, but when they see it spelt, they say Pearl-ta and all types of things.

It had been maybe a few months since I had seen my cousins Sara and Mick, and with one quick look at them, I realised that they had got manarta too. Mick looked like he had grown way bigger. Sara gave me a hug, and although I knew that Mick was a bit embarrassed about it, he gave me a hug too and said, "Pirlta Possum."

"Nhiina wanypatha?" they asked.
(Are you well?)

"Tyukarti, ngayi wanypatha," I replied.
(Yes, I'm good.)

After we said hello to everyone, Ngami asked me, "Do you want to go off with your cousins and explore around the camp?"

I ran off with my cousins to check out what was around us – the beach with all the mangroves not far away, sand dunes and lots of areas with trees with little yirtas (birds) flying all around the place.

When we had climbed to the top of one of the sand dunes, Sara asked, "Do you want to go swimming?" and of course, I said, "Sure, but I'll just ask Mum."

I ran back to the camp with my cousins and called out to Ngami, "Can I go swimming?"

"As long as you put on your hat and rashie and sunscreen," she said.

YIRTAS

After I had got changed, Sara and Mick stood giggling and whispering to each other while Ngami put sunscreen all over me.

Mick was carrying a big esky, and I asked, "What's that for?" and he said, "It's to collect things we find."

"Like what?" I asked, and he said, "Wapma," (snake) with a sneaky grin, and I said, "Nyuntyi," (liar) because our people don't eat snake. Snake is our big totem, it would be like eating our relatives.

"Off you go," Ngami said, and then she yelled out, "Kaltitya marnarta purlka," (listen to your big cousins) as we dashed toward the beach.

Chapter 2

Teasing Possum

When we were walking close to the shore Sara said, "Let's go swimming in the saltwater creek," and Mick said to Sara, "She's too nhuki mutlha." I know what mutlha means, it means nose, but I had no idea what nhuki means, and I asked, "What are you calling me?"

"Oh, nothing," Sara said. "Mick is just saying that you're too young to go in the creek, it's too deep."

"Yep, that's right, nhuki mutlha," he said with a giggle, and I wished that I knew more Nukunu warrarla (language). *What does nhuki mean?* I asked myself.

We got to a deep pool in the saltwater creek surrounded by mangroves.

Although I didn't think it was too deep for me, Sara wouldn't let me swim in it. But Sara and Mick got in. I sat there for a while watching them have all the fun swimming. I wasn't having any fun at all. I was bored. So I decided to explore the mangroves.

Suddenly I found myself sinking into mud and I had to reach onto a mangrove branch to pull myself out of it.

When I went back to the waterhole, Mick said, "Thungka thitna" and again I know what thitna is, it means feet, but I couldn't remember what thungka is.

"What are you calling me?" I asked, and Sara said, "Oh, nothing, Mick just said let's go crabbing."

I know what blue swimmer crabs are, they're yirityi, my favourite food, they taste heavenly.

I was glad to dip my feet into the shallows of the ocean as we started looking for yirityi, because the black-and-green mud that stuck to them really stank.

When we were in the shallows, we looked for black spots in the white sand where the yirityi had buried themselves. We poked the spots with sticks and sometimes the yirityi would pop up from beneath the sand. Sometimes the yirityi could be seen walking across the sand or trying to hide beneath the seaweed.

When I poked the second black hole that I saw, a yirityi sprang out of the sand and raised its claws to the sky as it shuffled backwards to try and get away from me. But I pounced on it, grabbed it on the back of its shell and put it into the esky.

YIRITYI

Maybe because I love yirityi so much,
I didn't care if they were to bite me when
we chased after them in the shallows
of the ocean. I was catching a lot more
yirityi than Sara and Mick were, and
after I'd caught five big ones and they'd
only caught two, Mick said to Sara, "She's
karntu-pirkinya mara."

I know what mara means, it means
hand, but I couldn't remember what
pirkinya means. I was sure that Mick
was teasing me, calling me something like
big hands.

"What are you calling me?" I asked, and again Sara replied, "Oh, nothing."

I was sure they were teasing me.

The yirityi got harder to catch as the tide started to come in. I realised that the water was almost up to my knees, and then Mick said, "The tide is coming in, we better get nhuki mutlha back to camp."

I knew Mick was teasing me and I was getting so mad and wished I knew more Nukunu warrarla, but I was also excited to show Ngami and Maama and the rest of our family all of the yirityi we'd caught and to cook them up and eat them.

When we got back to camp, Uncle Jack was already boiling up water on the fire to cook up all the yummy yirityi. When they were cooked, Uncle Jack placed them back in the esky to let them cool down for eating later.

Chapter 3

Aunty Janey Helps Out

I lay down in my tent wanting to get a little rest after all of the walking looking for yirityi. I couldn't really rest though, because I was mad that Mick and Sara were teasing me.

So, I thought about a plan to find out what they were saying. I couldn't just ask Ngami and Maama what Mick and Sara were saying, in case they were saying something really bad and Ngami and Maama got really angry. I didn't want my cousins to get into trouble.

I knew what to do, I'd ask Aunty Janey because she was always calm. Aunty Janey was also wanting to tell me stories about the purtlis (stars).

When it got dark, I asked Aunty Janey, "Can you tell me some stories about the purtlis?" and, as expected, Aunty Janey walked me out into the darkness, away from camp.

But just before she was about to launch into a story, I said, "Aunty Janey, I think Sara and Mick were teasing me."

"What do you mean you *think* they were teasing you?" asked Aunty Janey. "What happened while you were all exploring today?"

"Well, Sara and Mick were calling me things in Nukunu warrarla and I didn't know some of the words."

"What did they call you, little Pirlta?" Aunty Janey asked.

"Well, when we were walking to the waterhole Mick called me nhuki mutlha," I told her. "I know mutlha means nose but what is nhuki?"

Aunty Janey answered, "Nhuki means snot, Mick was calling you snotty nose."

I got mad and said, "But I haven't got a snotty nose."

"I know that," Aunty Janey said, "but it's just their way of saying you're their little cousin, because you know how little kids sometimes have snotty noses?"

"Oh," I said. "So Mick was really trying to be nice by calling me something bad?"

"Tyukarti! Yes!" Aunty Janey replied. "And what else did your cousins call you?" she asked.

"They called me thungka thitna, too," I told her.

"And what happened before they called you thungka thitna?" she asked.

I thought back and remembered sinking into the black-and-green mud, and then I told Aunty Janey about it.

"Did the mud stink?" she asked, and I said, "Tyukarti, it stank!"

"Well, thungka means stinking and they were calling you stinking feet," Aunty Janey told me. I thought about it and thought, *That's not so bad, my feet were stinking.*

"What about when they were calling me karntu-pirkinya mara? I mean I know what mara means, it means hands, but what about karntu-pirkinya?"

"What were you doing when they were calling you this?" Aunty Janey asked.

I said, "I was catching crabs."

"You caught the biggest mob of crabs didn't you, more than Sara and Mick?"

"Tyukarti!" I replied proudly.

"Well, my little Pirlta, they were calling you lightning hands!"

"Lightning hands?!" I asked, with a big smile spreading across my face.

"Tyukarti!" Aunty Janey said.

Chapter 4

Learning My Language

I stood beneath all the beautiful purtlis with Aunty Janey, thinking about how my big cousins were kind of being nice rather than really teasing me, but still thought, *I need to learn more Nukunu warrarla.*

I asked Aunty Janey, "How do I learn more Nukunu warrarla?"

She said, "You think about some ways to do that little Pirlta, and let me know what you think in the morning. Now, let's go and eat yirityi."

As soon as I heard those two words together, eat and yirityi, I almost forgot all about learning more Nukunu warrarla.

The next morning I was walking around with Ngami and Aunty Janey looking for bush tucker, berries and seeds. Aunty Janey asked, "So, what plan did you come up with for learning more Nukunu warrarla?"

I stopped and thought again about the things I'd come up with. "First, I'm going to teach some of my friends in the city some Nukunu words so that I can practise and remember speaking Nukunu. I will put a list of words in my room and sticky notes naming things around the house. And finally, can you please organise some language classes for us?"

Aunty Janey was smiling and said, "They're all great ideas and I'd love to start some language classes."

When I wanted to go crabbing with Sara and Mick later in the day, when the tide was low, I asked them, "Want to come crabbing with snotty nose, stinky feet, lightning hands?" and we all started laughing together.

Like always, I was sad to leave my Nukunu Country with Ngami and Maama. Especially when I got a big hug from Aunty Janey and she said, "Nhakutya nhiina Pirlta, see you Possum."